Quality-of-Life Financial Planning

A Life-Cycle Planning Approach

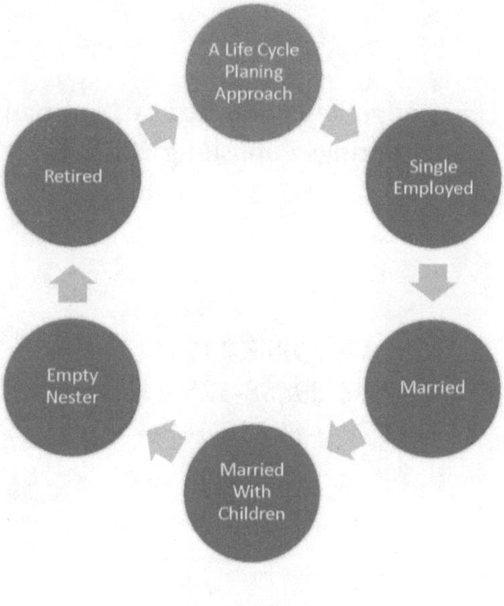

Dan Corbin

First Edition

NEWMAN SPRINGS PUBLISHING
Meadville, PA

First originally published by Newman
Springs Publishing 2025

ISBN 979-8-89888-117-7 (Paperback)
ISBN 979-8-89888-125-2 (Hardcover)
ISBN 979-8-89888-118-4 (Digital)

Printed in the United States of America

To my client base, friends, and business associates who encouraged me to share my quality-of-life financial planning process

Introduction

What drives people to overburden themselves with debt or spend more than they can afford? How does someone reach retirement age with little or no money saved? Why do people constantly create financial conflicts between what they want and what they can afford? How does a person who has made hundreds of millions of dollars end up bankrupt? Could it be as simple as these people are just financially wandering—wandering from one spending decision to another with no plan and no strategies or initiatives to enable the plan?

Dealing with personal finances is one of the leading stress factors in our society today. Financial misalignment between spouses is one of the leading causes of divorce today. Emotionally driven decisions based on what you want versus what you can afford are financially paralyzing people. Short-term thinking and planning are undermining longer-term results.

We do not teach people personal financial planning in high school. You will not learn it in college either unless you become a certified financial planner (CFP).

Many of my new clients think they have a plan, but they cannot tell me how they are going to execute the plan. Simply, they do not have strategies and initiatives aligned to support the plan. *What they really have is an idea.*

Some of my clients insist they have a plan, but their strategies and initiatives continue to fall short of enabling the plan. *What they really have is a dream.*

Repeatedly, I see clients focused on short-term budgets, only to watch them unravel. They lack a longer-term vision, and in turn, their financial decision-making has very little strategic content. Eventually, managing their finances becomes stressful, leaving many with feelings of frustration or hopelessness.

It Starts with a Plan

When people lay out their quality-of-life plan, they create a powerful vision that excites and guides them in their financial decision-making. In turn, their financial strategies and initiatives become more purposeful and disciplined. They move away from a restrictive-budget mindset to a proactive, longer-term execution focus. Their financial scorecard is simplified to enable a few quality-of-life plans across various life-cycle phases. The idea that they are the champions of their quality-of-life plans encourages them to make mindful decisions, be accountable, and continue educating themselves. Their quest is not financial planning perfection; rather, they build and continuously refine their road map of strategic sensibility.

I built my first financial plan when I was twenty-three years old. I built it to enable my simple quality-of-life plan at the time. I planned my annual cash flows so I could save money for a down payment on a home, pursue my hobbies, enjoy time with my family and friends, and minimize financial stress. I started contributing to my workplace pretax investment plan. I calculated the future values of my investment accounts with a plan to retire by age sixty-two.

Just for a frame of reference, in 1980 a cell phone would not fit in my full-size pickup glove box. There were no smartphones. There were no laptops. Corporate computers did not have the computing horsepower of today's smartphones. There were no apps. Microsoft Excel was still a decade away from launching. Social media consisted of the library, newspapers, magazines, TVs, radios, and talking to people face-to-face.

I created the time-consuming updated plans for the next decade on notebook paper, with a mechanical pencil and my trusty Texas Instruments calculator. In hindsight, the darn thing was not worth the paper I wrote it on a year later. However, it provided a directional set of indicators that kept me vested and excited and encouraged me to adjust when necessary. My investments are on track. My annual cash flows are on track to enable my quality-of-life plan. I also have sufficient contingency funds available to handle unexpected expenses. Alternatively, I need to revise my strategies and initiatives to enable or reenable my quality-of-life plan.

It would remain a very dynamic process for future years of planning. Most of the time, the adjustments were just timing changes related to shifting expenses or income. Other times, my quality-of-life plan evolved, requiring me to rethink my strategies and initiatives. This was especially true when I got married and my wife already had a child.

Fast-forward forty-five years, and I will tell you not much has changed. Sometimes you are financially on pace. Sometimes you are lagging. Sometimes you are ahead. As I said before, it is not about having a perfect plan. It is about having a good sensibility outlook to enable your quality-of-life plan. It is about creating a vision that excites and encourages you to make decisions that enable your plan. It is about updating your strategies and initiatives to drive plan execution. It is about continuing to learn and building a team of advisors to validate and refine your strategies.

This planning process is what I did every day at work as a business executive. We were constantly planning, defining strategies and initiatives to enable the plan, and measuring and tracking our results. The process was very dynamic, and continuous improvement was at the forefront of our strategic intentions. Sometimes the business environment changed so fast that we were working on revisions before we ever implemented strategies we constructed last month.

There are no crystal balls in the business or personal financial planning world. The realignment of strategies and initiatives to keep the plan on track is a dynamic process. *Your attitude about driving results is far more important than the financial plan itself.* The plan will evolve many times during your quality-of-life journey. You are going to have plan setbacks. You are going to have periods where the plan is overachieved. *If you can mentally accept that fact, you are way ahead of most people.*

It was natural for me to apply my business experiences to my personal financial planning process. As technology improved, so did the speed and ease of updating the financial plans. However, the process did not change. It was a quality-of-life plan sitting over the top of my financial strategies, initiatives, and decision-making.

I was dictatorially the champion of my quality-of-life plan, just like every great CEO I worked with was the champion of their company's business plans and strategies. CEOs use their management team, board of directors, consultants, and other resources as soundboards for strategic development. Successful clients build their advisor team to do the same. *Successful CEOs have skilled management teams to delegate key initiatives and execute strategies and initiatives. Successful champions of their quality-of-life plans? No such luck.*

Over the past forty-five years, there have been several major events that made me rethink my financial strategies and initiatives. Some of those were positive deviations (e.g., workplace raises, promotions, workplace bonuses, stock options or grants, and higher-than-planned rate of returns on investments). Some of them were negative deviations (e.g., recessions or poor marketplace returns, high inflation, unforeseen major expenses, loss of joint income sooner than expected when the children arrived, changes in tax laws, changes in regulations, and increasing tax liabilities). Some of them were just timing influences (e.g., a rapid increase in expenses when I got married and had a stepson on the same day, workplace wage freezes, relocation to a new state, and uncertainty with expenses related to adopting our children).

I can tell you my quality-of-life plan has not changed drastically over the past four decades, but there was definitely constant fine-tuning of the strategies to enable it. Most of that tuning was to enable a quality-of-life plan for my wife and our children.

I always knew I wanted to be married, and I wanted children. I wanted to pay for my children's education and buy them their first car. I wanted to be financially independent at retirement age. I wanted to travel and enjoy vacations with family and friends. I wanted to pursue my hobbies. What I wanted really did not change that much over the decades, but how much it cost sure did.

I will tell you most people are ill prepared to develop a personal financial plan. Not only are young people entering the workforce unprepared, but many people who have been working for years cannot craft a reasonable financial plan.

Today, when I talk to younger people about financial planning, I usually get "Oh yeah, I do that on my app."

I just smile, resisting telling them that tracking income, investment accounts, and expenses is vastly different from having a set of financial strategies and initiatives that enables a quality-of-life plan. *They might know what the score is, but most do not have a clue what game they are playing.*

I see employees with stock options or stock grants who have no idea how to value them. They do not understand the tax implications of exercising or selling them.

I see employees underinvesting in their workplace pretax savings plan. They simply do not know how to create a vision of the future value potential of their investments. The power of compound interest is not in their field of vision. They lack the understanding that time is their ally when they start investing early in life, and their nemesis if they wait too long.

I see people participating in workplace pretax investment plans with little to no strategic intention. Perhaps their focus is on achieving a number. The number could be an investment portfolio balance at a defined age or before retirement. They do not stop to ask themselves, "Why am I doing this, and what is the strategic benefit of reaching the number?"

The answer should be "It enables my quality-of-life plan."

I see people with high debt levels and no understanding of how much interest they are paying or how much longer it will continue. Trapped in the spiderweb of their own unconscious spending habits, they continue to pursue what they want versus what they can afford. Poor debt management is the number one factor that can—and will—derail your quality-of-life plans.

I see people making premature decisions on the year they will retire and the year they will take Social Security. Most often they allowed others to drive their strategies and resent it later (family, friends, financial advisors, tax advisors, and social media influencers, among others).

When I provide clients with a financial plan framework, the intention is to help them in the pursuit of *their* quality-of-life plan. We overlay strategies and initiatives to enable the plan. We explore strategic alternatives. We create a vision of financial key indicators for a sensibility check. We build a directional road map for execution. We build a team of advisors, and we seek out and encourage input from that team.

The plans are custom plans because no two clients have the same quality-of-life plan, and their sources of income vary. Some clients have pretax investment plans. Some after-tax investment plans. Some have both. Some have annuities. Some have pensions. Some clients have rental income; and some have stock options, stock grants, or stock they own outright.

While there is no template that covers all clients, there are macro-level financial indicators that almost all my clients need to understand. It does not matter what life cycle stage you are currently in, how old you are, how much money you make, or how much your net worth is.

Key Financial Indicators

1. Are my investments on track to support my quality-of-life plans long-term as I transition through future life-cycle phases?
2. What are my spending ratios as a percentage of my net income, and what is the outlook in future years?
3. Do my plans include future expenses to maintain and replenish the things I have today or will need to afford as I transition through future life-cycle phases (e.g., cars, home down payment and mortgage, home maintenance, child-rearing expenses, vacations, and changes in income if one spouse stops working when the children arrive)?
4. When unexpected expenses or loss of income happens, do I have reasonable contingency funds available?
5. If I exhaust my contingency funds, how long will it take me to replenish them?
6. Will I run out of money before I die? (No one knows when he or she is going to die, so we encourage our clients to plan beyond their statistical life expectancy.)
7. Is my plan for retirement sensible?

I am not going to tell you that you need to invest *x* percentage of your income. I am not going to tell you that you have to track every dollar you spend. I am not going to tell you that your contingency funds need to cover *y* months of your expenses. I am not going to tell you the best age to retire, take Social Security, or insist you follow other strategies.

I focus on providing strategic options and being a resource to help you enable your quality-of-life plan. I provide coaching and continuing education so you make informed decisions.

I will simply leave it at this: You have to be the champion of your strategies and initiatives to enable your vision of a quality-of-life plan.

Life Cycle Planning

Single and employed. We all start our financial journey in this life-cycle phase. Some of my clients remain single and employed until they transition to retirement. The fact that we are responsible for ourselves versus our spouse, children, or others may simplify our financial strategies and initiatives.

Married. This life-cycle phase often results in an increase in net income and a lower ratio of expense versus combined net income. It can be a tempting time to make major purchases (e.g., homes, vehicles, etc.). When clients make these major purchases with debt, it can derail them financially as they transition to the married-with-children stage.

Married with children. Other than retirement, this life-cycle stage will likely be the longest in terms of future years (you are legally responsible for children for eighteen years, realistically eighteen to twenty-two years). Most of us underestimate the real cost of raising our children. It is also a time when a spouse may stop working short- or longer-term to be home with their children. Regardless of whether both spouses are working or not, your expenses are likely increasing faster than your income at times during this life-cycle phase.

Empty nesters. The children are financially independent or significantly less dependent on Mom and Dad. Typically, Mom and Dad are in their peak earnings years. Expenses are dropping as a percentage of net income. Strategic decisions on retirement age, when to take Social Security, health insurance, and other factors are on your radar screen or should be. Making premature decisions on what year you will retire and when you file for Social Security is risky.

Retired—golden years. You may still have ordinary income, as some of my clients continue to work after taking Social Security. Most of my clients are living off fixed income from Social Security, pension plans, and investment income. Future years' cash flow analysis and sensitivity analysis are important. Careful planning for future expenses is important (e.g., home maintenance or upgrades, vehicles, health care, etc.).

It does not matter what life-cycle stage you are currently in or what stage you transition to next. A quality-of-life plan represents your unique life's journey. It is a vision of what is important to you.

Building Your Quality-of-Life Plan

Below is an example of a quality-of-life plan for someone who is single and employed, who plans to marry and have children. The plan will likely be refined many times in our life's journey.

Single and Employed	• Enjoy time with family and friends. • Pursue hobbies and join a golf club. • Take two vacations each year.
Married	• Take two vacations to the beach each year. • Pursue hobbies. • Enjoy time with family and friends. • Purchase a home.
Married with Children	• Take two family vacations each year. • Once spouse will stop working the first year each of our two children are born. • Upgrade to a larger family vehicle. • Limit financial stress.
Empty Nester	• Take 3-4 vacations each year. • More frequent entertainment enjoyment with family and friends. • Purchase a boat and enjoy time fishing and boating.
Retired	• Purchase a lakefront property. • Travel abroad. • Increase entertainment expenses—family and friends.

Planning Sensibility

Start with the life-cycle phase you are in now. Do not worry about perfection in planning. Think about it this way: Your quality-of-life plan should provide a vision for developing financial strategies and initiatives to enable the plan. Unless you are retired or quickly approaching retirement, you will need to revise your quality-of-life plan from time to time. Typically, for any given life-cycle stage, my clients have two to four quality-of-life plans.

You do not need to overthink plans for future life-cycle phases until you approach them. For example, if you are in your twenties, single, and employed and you have no immediate plans to marry, keep your future life-cycle plans directional and simple. Build strategies and initiatives to enable your quality of life for your current life-cycle phase and redefine or refine your future quality-of-life plans and strategies as soon as you plan to transition to the next life-cycle phase.

The one exception is retirement. As early as possible, you should have quality-of-life plans for this life-cycle phase. They may be very high-level plans to begin with. For example, I want to be financially independent at sixty-two. I want to enjoy time with family and friends. I want to pursue my hobbies. I want to travel more often. You need to enable your plans with investment strategies to support them. You need time to enable those strategies.

I also caution you not to wait until the last minute to define quality-of-life plans for future life-cycle phases. This is especially true as you approach the married-with-children life-cycle phase. This is a time when your expenses may be increasing faster than your income periodically. If a spouse is going to take time off work when the children arrive, you need time to develop cash flow strategies to support that choice. If you are going to send your children to private schools and pay for their college education, you need cash flow plans to support those strategies.

I further caution you to properly rationalize your debt and understand the impact it will have as you transition into future life-cycle phases. I constantly see clients who make major debt decisions, only to have it unravel their quality-of-life plans later. *I am not of the mindset that all debt is bad. I am of the mindset that debt must support, not diminish, your quality-of-life plans.*

Chasing Financial Targets

Often people communicate financial targets when setting up their quality-of-life plans. *If we define a quality-of-life plan by a set of financial metrics, we have the cart before the horse.* Below are a few examples:

Financial Goal	Quality-of-Life Plan
I want to be a millionaire before I retire.	I want to be financially independent by retirement age.
I want to spend $10,000 per year in retirement to travel.	I want to travel more often postretirement.
I want to buy a boat for $50,000.	I want to enjoy time on the water fishing with my family and friends.
I want to buy a $250,000 home before age thirty-two.	I want the comfort of owning a home before I have children.

Your quality-of-life plan needs to be visionary. Once the longer-term simple vision is in place, we can rationalize strategies and initiatives to enable the plan. There are no perfect strategies and initiatives to enable your quality-of-life plan. You will have multiple strategic options to consider.

Some of my clients tend to pursue financial targets with little to no alignment on how it enables their quality-of-life plans. When I ask them, "What is the significance of reaching your financial target?" they struggle to tell me. For example, a recent client wanted to have $1,500,000 saved for retirement at age sixty-six. I asked how they came up with the $1,500,000 number, and there was an awkward pause in the conversation. The final answer was "I think this will be a good amount."

My next question was "Could you enable your quality-of-life plan with less?"

"Not sure at this point."

"Would you like to find out?"

"Yes."

Your quality-of-life plan always sits on top of any financial strategies and initiatives, not vice versa.

Strategies

We need high-level strategies defined to enable our quality-of-life plan. Below is an example that supports the quality-of-life plan example. The strategies will likely change many times throughout your journey.

Stage	Strategies
Single and Employed	• Pay off debts. • Maximize contributions to investment accounts. • Build contingency funds. • Rationalize future expenses (e.g., vehicles, home purchase, and other major expenses).
Married	• Purchase a home with 20 percent down payment and 15-year fixed rate. • Build your team of advisors (legal, investment, tax, and insurance). • Increase focus on future expenses and understand cash flows. • Validate strategies with your team of advisors.
Married with Children	• Map out children-related and other future expenses. • Understand expenses trade-offs while one spouse is not working—cash flow strategies. • Update retirement outlook to assure investments are on track. • Validate strategies with your team of advisors.
Empty Nester	• Increase contribution to investment accounts for retirement. • Increase focus on cash flow analysis for retirement years. • Pay off mortgage after updating cash flow models. • Rationalize options for lake home purchase, and validate strategies with your team of advisors.
Retired	• Understand cash flow outlook and options to maximize your retirement. • Rationalization of future expenses important (e.g., vehicles, home repairs, travel, and insurance). • Validate strategies with your team of advisors.

Initiatives

Think about strategies versus initiatives like this: Strategies are *what* you need to do to enable your plan, while initiatives are *how* you are going to execute the strategies. Below is a simple list of initiatives that support the quality-of-life plan strategies.

Life Stage	Initiatives
Single and Employed	• Pay off the car in future year-end 1. • Build up contingency funds to a minimum of 6 months' expenses once the car is paid off. • Increase contributions to pretax investment plan once contingency funds are in place. • Model cash flow outlook for next 3-5 years and renew annually. • Model long-term investments outlook for retirement.
Married	• Save $45K for home down payment and closing costs. • Explore and determine advisor-team priorities. • Map out future expenses, including the early years of raising children. • Model cash flow outlook for next 3-5 year and renew annually.
Married with Children	• Refine cash flow outlook for next 5-10 years and renew annually. • Build up contingency funds to support increasing future expenses. • Explore strategic options for future expenses with your team of advisors.
Empty Nester	• Map out your retirement cash flow outlook and review annually with your advisors. • Explore options on the timing of mortgage payoff and future lake house purchase. • Run a sensitivity analysis on marketplace downturns and inflation during the early years of retirement if you need income from your investment accounts to cover annual expenses.
Retired	• Define your life expectancy and model cash flows annually for review with your advisor team. • Make sure your living wills, trusts, and other legal documents are updated as necessary. • Start planning your wealth pass on strategies using your team of advisors.

Executing the Plan

The goal of your financial strategies and initiatives should be to enable your quality-of-life plans. You are going to have to overcome hurdles along the way, many of which will not be totally in your control. Laws and regulations change. Unexpected loss of income and unexpected major expenses will require you to rethink your strategies and initiatives. The investment markets go up, and they go down. The timing of when they go up or down may require you to adjust your strategies and initiatives.

The goal is not to have a perfect financial plan, which is impractical. The goal is to have a renewable process that can quickly adapt when the unexpected arrives. The goal is to create a strategic road map to keep your quality-of-life plans on track. Financial key indicator reports should provide a blueprint for your longer-term quality-of-life plan sensibility, allowing you to adjust when necessary. Shorter-term execution on the strategies and initiatives will be your major responsibility to assure that you do not create conflicts with your quality-of-life plan.

Think about strategies just like a road map (not today's GPS mapping programs). For those of you under the age of forty, you may need to pause a second and look up what a road map or road atlas is. These are the tools your parents and generations before used to travel from point A to point B. When point B was a new destination that required navigating roads that we may or may not be familiar with, it was our strategic blueprint.

My plan is to go from my hometown in Ohio to Iowa City, Iowa. The route appears straightforward: Travel north for about an hour to Toledo, Ohio, and get on I-80 West. Stay on I-80 West until I get to the Iowa City exit. Strategy established.

I have a plan: Travel to Iowa City. I have a strategy—my route to get there. I have some initiatives linked to the strategy. I want to arrive the day I leave by late afternoon. I will leave early, as snow is in the forecast. I will plan the trip to avoid rush hour afternoon traffic in Chicago.

Plan—complete. ☑

Strategies—complete. ☑

Key initiatives—complete. ☑

I made this trip in November 1981, my first of many. I made it to Iowa City, but not the way I planned. Let us look at what happened.

It was smooth sailing for the first ninety minutes. It had started to snow earlier than forecasted, but it was manageable. And there were no major delays. I stopped for gas in Indiana near the Illinois border.

Back on the road about ten minutes later, traffic came to a dead stop. Forty-five minutes later (about a mile down the road), I was forced to exit the highway and take a detour, as there was a major truck accident ahead that was blocking all lanes. My plan was unchanged. My strategy needed revision. That change in strategy would affect my initiatives.

Eventually (about ninety minutes behind schedule), I was getting back on I-80 West. Thereafter, I was approaching the Chicago city limits. It was there and then that I learned there is no rush hour in Chicago. Chicago has rush *hours*; I was even further behind my trip plan.

Fast-forward about an hour, and Chicago was in my rearview mirror (not that I could see it, as I was going snow-blind from heavy blowing flakes). I was traveling about fifty miles per hour in heavy traffic with road conditions getting worse by the minute. Fast-forward several hours later, and I was nearing the Iowa City exit. I was hours behind my initial plan for arrival.

Did I accomplish my plan? Yes, but not with the strategies and initiatives I had laid out. Financial planning is no different. You will see many curveballs in your journey. You will be hit by more than one pitch. You are going to have to play some extra innings if you want to win. Understand this: There are very few perfect strategies and initiatives to enable your quality-of-life plan. Stay flexible, proactive, and dynamic in your financial planning journey.

Process Summary

1. Create your quality-of-life plan.
2. Draft your financial strategies to enable the plan.
3. Define your key initiatives to support your strategies.
4. Focus on shorter-term execution (e.g., next year or two) and react quickly when unexpected changes in income or expenses occur.
5. Renew your long-term financial outlooks when sensible (e.g., major changes in quality-of-life plans, income, expenses, investment portfolio, or change in life-cycle phase).
6. Build your team of advisors and use them to develop, refine, and validate your strategies and initiatives. This team will be a continuing education forum for you and will keep you up to speed on changes in laws and regulations. Engage people who have a sincere interest in helping you achieve your quality-of-life plan. Avoid people who want to dictate your strategy and tell you how to behave.
7. Repeat steps 1–6 above as necessary.

Characteristics of Successful Clients

1. They have a *simple* but *renewable* vision of their quality-of-life plan.
2. They have *high-level strategies defined* to enable the plan.
3. They have *key initiatives defined to support their strategies* and drive shorter-term execution.
4. The strategies and initiatives function as a road map for plan execution (debt decisions, investment decisions, spending decisions). Their spending decisions *enable their quality-of-life plan.*
5. They are *adaptable to change* and react quickly when unplanned events affect them. They accept the fact that they cannot control every financial event that affects their quality-of-life plans. They react quickly when life throws them a curveball.
6. *They are curious.* They explore financial options, educate themselves on changes in laws and regulations, as well as other factors that can affect their plans. They embrace

having a team of advisors and encourage their input.

7. They are the *champions* of their plan execution. They are likely to have a team of advisors; but they never allow others to control their plan, strategies, or initiatives.
8. They have *visionary intentions*. They do not worry about having a perfect plan because they understand they will never be in control of all the environmental influences that can affect their plans. They have directional strategic intentions that are renewable. They are thinking and planning beyond the short term.

Short-Term Budgets

Short-term budgets are helpful for executing a short-term plan. Yes, we must manage the short term. The idea that you can budget every penny you are spending, even for the next month, is challenging. The challenge increases when you get married and increases again when you have children. The challenge increases when we increase the number of things we own that have to be maintained or replaced. Unexpected expenses come up that you cannot accurately plan. Nobody knows the date and time that their car is going to break down, the heater or AC unit is going to fail, the day your child is injured, or other unplanned events surface. However, that does not mean we cannot have contingency plans to prepare for the unknown.

Within reason and control, and inside the bounds of a quality-of-life plan, we can be modestly spontaneous in our spending decisions (e.g., stopping for ice cream, going out to eat with friends, or going to an entertainment event). The problems begin to surface when we create conflicts between our quality-of-life plan and our spending decisions. It is easy to create strategic conflicts when you focus on short-term budgets. You need a longer-term simple set of financial indicators and cash flow outlooks to enable a quality-of-life plan.

I *never* tell my clients what their quality-of-life plan should be. I help them understand the sensibility of their plan. I help them enable those plans with sound financial planning and coaching. I encourage them to think longer term. I provide them with strategic options to enable their quality-of-life plan. Sometimes coaching is not so much about what a client wants to do but more about if, when, and how they will be able to do it.

Once we complete aligning strategies and initiatives to the various life-cycle phases, the execution focuses on the shorter term. The visionary focus creates an understanding of what actions are required to support the overall quality-of-life plan. The longer-term cash flow outlooks encourage strategic decisions or timing of spending decisions, especially major future expenses such as home mortgages, cars, home maintenance, and child-rearing expenses, among others.

A Word of Caution

There is an abundance of information available today to consider in your financial planning journey. Social media influencers are promoting content on almost any financial question you could ask. You can read many books. Financial advisors have their scripts of how you should move forward. Retirement planners have the "fourth-grade math" lined up to convince you that this is the best strategy for retirement age, taking Social Security, and other recommendations. Just remember two things as you move forward:

1. Thinking is a prerequisite to learning. If you blindly adopt strategies from others, get ready to call a tow truck when your plan crashes.
2. When anyone tells you, "This is the best or only strategy," proceed with extreme caution. Take the following as examples:

    a. You should take Social Security at age *x*.
    b. You need *x* amount of money before you retire.

c. You should pay off your home before retirement.
d. Paying off your home mortgage early is a poor financial strategy.
e. You should have an emergency fund of *x*.
f. This investment vehicle is better than that investment vehicle.
g. You should be investing *x* in your employer pretax savings plans.

It frightens me when I listen to most social media advice on finance or books I have read. At best, it is blind advice from supposed experts in their fields. It is blind advice when someone pretends that it covers all people and situations and when they do not link those strategies to a client's quality-of-life plan. At worst, it is simply bad advice.

In my business career, I have come across several people claiming they are experts in their field. Many of these people are confused about the difference between being an expert versus having experience.

After watching Tiger Woods bounce balls off the face of his iron between his legs and around his back early in his PGA career, I thought, *Cool, I am going to do that.* I went to the range, and about three minutes in, I hit my kneecap with my sand wedge. It was a very unpleasant experience. Hobbling back to the clubhouse, I now had experience bouncing a golf ball off the face of my iron. No one at the driving range made the mistake of thinking I was an expert.

People also confuse doing something for a long period with being an expert. The problem is many of them are doing the same thing, the same way today, as they did the first day on the job. No doubt, they have experience. The jury is still out on their level of expertise.

And so it is in the financial planning landscape. There are people out there who have years of experience. There are people out there who are still doing the same thing today that they did years or decades ago. They have their degrees and title acronyms proudly displayed on their office walls. They could be financial coaches, authors, financial advisors, retirement advisors, or CPAs. They have their process outlined and encourage you to follow along, the great majority of which promotes the idea that you should do A, B, C, or D.

Most of this content centers on two fallacies. First, the idea that doing A, B, C, or D is the best option for you. Second, the idea that you have to behave in a certain manner or reach some arbitrary financial target to enable your quality-of-life plan. Be careful when you build your team of financial advisors. Be careful whose advice you consider.

I see social media influencers and others guiding people on how to become a millionaire, oftentimes with recommendations that undermine their quality-of-life journey along the way. What is the point? "Hurray, I am a millionaire and retired, but I had to endure a poor or substandard quality of life to achieve it." Statistically, more than two-thirds of your life is over if you retire at age sixty-two.

These same people are studying and characterizing how millionaires behave, trying to convince you that you need to follow a similar path. No one is talking about the nonmillionaires who are enjoying a high quality of life before and during retirement. There are a lot more of these people than there are millionaires. I have many clients who enjoy a high quality of life during retirement who are not millionaires.

Never let anyone drive your financial strategies. That is reserved for you, the CEO of your quality-of-life plan.

Building Your Advisor Team

Your advisors need to be a resource to help you with enabling your quality-of-life plans, not dictating your strategies. If you blindly adopt their strategies and input, you have just given up partial control of your quality-of-life plan. Your advisor team should offer strategic input that lays out options for financial decisions, add sensibility to your financial assumptions if necessary, and focus on educating you so you make informed decisions. Their job is to be a resource to their clients.

Your job is to ask for input so you make informed decisions and continue to learn. You want a team that can play devil's advocate so you can test and validate strategies, not someone who is going to tell you what they think you want to hear. You want a team that can run sensitivity analysis on key plan assumptions. You want a team that can help you react when the unknown surfaces. This is an important step in your continuing education process and in optimizing your evolving strategies.

I set my expectations right up front when I interview financial advisors. I tell them I have a plan that I want them to help me execute. I caution them that I am not going to allow them to drive my strategies but rather seek a partner to help me keep my quality-of-life plan on track and refined. I make those plans transparent right from the start. I am an open book with my quality-of-life plan, investment account balances, cash flow outlooks, and strategies.

I am looking for a team that is sincerely interested in helping me refine my strategies to enable my quality-of-life plans. I want a team that is very responsive if my plan changes.

Remember this: It is your quality-of-life plan. Your advisor team is simply a resource to assist you. Just like an employee at a company, their fundamental job is to bring a skill set you need so you can accomplish an objective. The fact is, if you had the time, skill, and knowledge to do it yourself, you would not need them.

Common Planning Misconceptions

1. *I do not make enough money to have a financial plan.* There are countless examples of people who accumulated wealth and had a high quality of life with modest income levels. How much money you make may limit how much discretionary spending you can afford, but it should not limit a reasonable quality-of-life plan.
2. *I do not have time to deal with a financial plan.* That thinking usually results in increasing financial stress down the road. People who wait too long to start their investment plans, or who create conflicts with their spending decisions, usually see the negative impacts later. The time they did not spend enabling their quality-of-life plan is oftentimes spent unraveling the messes they create with their short-term day-to-day spending decisions.
3. *I do not need any advisors or coach to assist me.* Do not underestimate the challenges that come with enabling your quality-of-life

plan. You may not need much assistance when you are single and employed and in your twenties, but preparing for life cycle changes down the road is beyond the financial planning logical aptitude of most people. Having a team of advisors to test, validate, and continue your financial education is valuable, especially when laws and regulations change.

4. *I do not know how to get started.* Commitment on your part is step 1! Step 2 is to lay out your quality-of-life plan. Step 3 is to find resources that can help you enable your quality-of-life plan. Step 4 is aligning strategies and initiatives to enable the plan. Step 5 is to accept the fact that this is a dynamic process. It requires your attention and effort moving forward.

A Common Theme

There are financial coaches who work with people who have riddled themselves with debt and are on a very poor financial path. I do not.

Almost all my new clients were on a reasonable trajectory financially; they just need guidance on strategic refinement, continuing education, and creating meaningful cash flow outlooks.

I ask all of my clients the same question: What is it that inspired you to behave the way you do with your financial decisions?

Very seldom did a client say, "I learned this from my parents or someone else." Rather, their financial decision-making centered on their vision of how they wanted to live their life.

Did they have a formal quality-of-life plan written down? Very few did, but they had an intuitive sensibility that guided them on their financial decision-making and behaviors ("I want to avoid financial stress, and I want to have enough money to retire comfortably," for example).

They saved money consistently, managed their expenses not frugally but sensibly, and were cautious with their debt decisions. They were always thinking ahead, and they understood what they could afford.

It did not matter how much money they made, what their net worth was, or how old they were. All of them had an intrinsic set of financial decision-making guidelines that acted as macro-level financial strategies to enable their quality-of-life plans. Their vision of how they wanted to live life was powerful, and they were undeniably the champions of their quality-of-life plan.

Less than half of these clients were millionaires or would be at retirement. Of these, most were on course to enable their quality-of-life plan well beyond their statistical life expectancy.

It is not about how much money you make. It is about behaving in a way that enables and enriches your quality of life.

Case Studies

The following case studies are from actual clients I have assisted. I have changed the clients' names to provide anonymity.

John and Mary

John and Mary were married last year. They are both thirty years old. They are living in an apartment but want to purchase a home within a year. They also want to start a family and raise two children in the near future. Mary wants to be a stay-at-home mom the first year after each child arrives.

Below is the quality-of-life plan they developed through the married-with-children life-cycle phase.

John & Mary Quality of Life Plan

Quality of Life Plan	Strategies	Initiatives
Married:		
Enjoy time with family and friends	Minimize financial stress. Prepare for future children related expenses. Save 20% for home down payment. Minimize debt.	Build cash flow outlooks for next 5 years.
Pursue our hobbies.		Forecast investments accounts balances long term.
Take two vacations each year.		Assure contingency funds are adequate.
Purchase a home.		Payoff vehicle debt.
Married with Children:		
Mary will stay at home the first year each child is born	Minimize financial stress. Minimize debt. Increase focus on retirement outlook.	Build cash flow outlooks for next 10 years.
Pursue our hobbies.		Create high level outlook of retirement cash flows.
Take two family vacations each year.		Assure contingency funds are adequate 5-10 years.
Enjoy time with family and friends.		Build our team of advisors.

Here is a snapshot of their current-year income and expenses. Both had been participating in their employer's pretax investment plan, contributing 15 percent of their gross income for the past seven years. At the beginning of the year, their combined pretax investment account balances were approaching $90,000. At the current year's beginning, they had $42,000 in their checking and savings accounts. Their expenses were 75 percent of their net income (take-home pay). At the end of the current year, their checking and savings account balance would be approaching $60,000, providing 13.4 months of contingency funds.

John & Mary Financial Example 1

Expense Type			Current Year
	Year begin combined checking & savings	$	42,000
	Home downpayment & closing costs		
	John Gross Income	$	52,000
	Marry Gross Income	$	50,000
	Combined Gross Income	**$**	**102,000**
	John Contribution to Pre-tax Investment Plan	$	7,800
	Marry Contribution to Pre-tax Investment Plan	$	7,500
	Combined Contributions to Pre-tax Investment Plans	**$**	**15,300**
	John Net income after tax withholdings	$	36,244
	Marry Net income after tax withholdings	$	34,850
	Combined Net Income after tax withholding	**$**	**71,094**
Expense Type	**Annual Expenses**		
Essential	Rent or Mortgage	$	16,800
Essential	Utilities	$	1,440
Essential	Insurances & Health Care	$	4,000
Essential	Groceries	$	12,000
Debt	Vehicle payments	$	12,000
Discretionary	Clothes	$	2,400
Discretionary	Entertainment	$	2,400
Discretionary	All other	$	2,400
	Total	**$**	**53,440**
	Net Income minus expenses (cash flow)	**$**	**17,654**
	Expenses % of net income		75%
	Essential expenses % of net income		48%
	Debt % of net income		17%
	Year end Checking & savings accounts	$	59,654
	Checking & Saving months of expense coverage		13.4

Below is the first draft of a three-year cash flow outlook plan we developed, assuming a home purchase in future year one and the arrival of their first child in future year two. As you can see, we had some challenges to resolve. Without Mary's income in year three, their checking and savings balance was negative at year-end, leaving them with no contingency funds. They also were not making further contributions to their investment plans. Back to the drawing board—this cash flow outlook does not support their quality-of-life plan. We needed to rethink the strategies to see if we could enable their quality-of-life plan.

John & Mary Financial Example 2

Expense Type		Current	Future Year 1 - After Home Purchase	Future Year 2 After Child Birth
	Year begin combined checking & savings	$ 42,000	$ 59,654	$ 21,125
	Home downpayment & closing costs		$ 45,000	
	John Gross Income	$ 52,000	$ 53,560	$ 55,167
	Marry Gross Income	$ 50,000	$ 51,500	
	Combined Gross Income	**$ 102,000**	**$ 105,060**	**$ 55,167**
	John Contribution to Pre-tax Investment Plan	$ 7,800	$ 8,034	$ -
	Marry Contribution to Pre-tax Investment Plan	$ 7,500	$ 7,725	$ -
	Combined Contributions to Pre-tax Investment Plans	**$ 15,300**	**$ 15,759**	**$ -**
	John Net income after tax withholdings	$ 36,244	$ 37,331	$ 45,237
	Marry Net income after tax withholdings	$ 34,850	$ 35,896	$ -
	Combined Net Income after tax withholding	**$ 71,094**	**$ 73,227**	**$ 45,237**
Expense Type	**Annual Expenses**			
Essential	Rent or Mortgage	$ 16,800	$ 24,780	$ 24,780
Essential	Utilities	$ 1,440	$ 3,000	$ 3,090
Essential	Insurances & Health Care	$ 4,000	$ 7,200	$ 8,280
Essential	Groceries	$ 12,000	$ 12,360	$ 15,450
Debt	Vehicle payments	$ 12,000	$ 12,000	$ 12,000
Discretionary	Clothes	$ 2,400	$ 2,472	$ 1,236
Discretionary	Entertainment	$ 2,400	$ 2,472	$ 1,236
Discretionary	All other	$ 2,400	$ 2,472	$ 1,236
	Total	**$ 53,440**	**$ 66,756**	**$ 67,308**
	Net Income minus expenses (cash flow)	**$ 17,654**	**$ 6,471**	**$ (22,071)**
	Expenses % of net income	75%	91%	149%
	Essential expenses % of net income	48%	65%	114%
	Debt % of net income	17%	16%	27%
	Year end Checking & savings accounts	$ 59,654	$ 21,125	$ (946)
	Checking & Saving months of expense coverage	13.4	3.8	(0.2)

We decided to expand the cash flow model to five years. We assumed that the second child would be born within this period. The clients did not want to delay the purchase of their home. Mary was standing firm on her desire to stay at home for one year after each child was born.

We ran multiple cash flow scenarios with varying strategies. John and Mary chose the following.

John and Mary would reduce their contribution to their workplace pretax plans to 7.5 percent for the next three years. They would start investing at a rate of 15 percent or greater again in future years three to five (of course, Mary could not invest in the years she was staying home with the children—years three and five). They also decided to pay off their vehicle loans before the beginning of future year two. Discretionary spending would be reduced by 50 percent to maintain a reasonable level of contingency funds for unexpected expenses. We estimated future expenses and used inflation factors for future years. We were conservative in our assumptions about wage increases year over year. Now we had a set of strategies and initiatives that could enable their plan.

John & Mary Financial Example 3

Expense Type		Current	Future Year 1 - After Home Purchase	Future Year 2 After Child Birth	Future Year 3 Both Spouse Working	Future Year 4 Both Spouse Working	Future Year 5 After 2nd Child Birth
	Year begin combined checking & savings	$ 42,000	$ 65,927	$ 30,175	$ 16,819	$ 32,499	$ 49,392
	Home downpayment & closing costs		$ 45,000				
	John Gross Income	$ 52,000	$ 53,560	$ 55,167	$ 56,822	$ 58,526	$ 60,282
	Marry Gross Income	$ 50,000	$ 51,500		$ 51,500	$ 53,045	
	Combined Gross Income	**$ 102,000**	**$ 105,060**	**$ 55,167**	**$ 108,322**	**$111,571**	**$ 60,282**
	John Contribution to Pre-tax Investment Plan	$ 3,900	$ 4,017	$ 4,138	$ 8,523	$ 8,779	$ 4,521
	Marry Contribution to Pre-tax Investment Plan	$ 3,750	$ 3,863	$ -	$ 7,725	$ 7,957	$ -
	Combined Contributions to Pre-tax Investment Plans	**$ 7,650**	**$ 7,880**	**$ 4,138**	**$ 16,248**	**$ 16,736**	**$ 4,521**
	John Net income after tax withholdings	$ 39,442	$ 40,625	$ 41,844	$ 39,605	$ 40,793	$ 45,724
	Marry Net income after tax withholdings	$ 37,925	$ 39,063	$ -	$ 35,896	$ 36,972	$ -
	Combined Net Income after tax withholding	**$ 77,367**	**$ 79,688**	**$ 41,844**	**$ 75,500**	**$ 77,765**	**$ 45,724**
Expense Type	**Annual Expenses**						
Essential	Rent or Mortgage	$ 16,800	$ 24,780	$ 24,780	$ 24,780	$ 24,780	$ 24,780
Essential	Utilities	$ 1,440	$ 3,000	$ 3,090	$ 3,183	$ 3,278	$ 3,377
Essential	Insurances & Health Care	$ 4,000	$ 7,200	$ 8,280	$ 8,528	$ 8,784	$ 9,048
Essential	Groceries	$ 12,000	$ 12,360	$ 15,450	$ 15,914	$ 16,391	$ 20,489
Debt	Vehicle payments	$ 12,000	$ 19,500	$ -			
Discretionary	Clothes	$ 2,400	$ 1,200	$ 1,200	$ 2,472	$ 2,546	$ 2,801
Discretionary	Entertainment	$ 2,400	$ 1,200	$ 1,200	$ 2,472	$ 2,546	$ 2,623
Discretionary	All other	$ 2,400	$ 1,200	$ 1,200	$ 2,472	$ 2,546	$ 2,623
	Total	**$ 53,440**	**$ 70,440**	**$ 55,200**	**$ 59,821**	**$ 60,872**	**$ 65,739**
	Net Income minus expenses (cash flow)	**$ 23,927**	**$ 9,248**	**$ (13,356)**	**$ 15,680**	**$ 16,893**	**$ (20,015)**
	Expenses % of net income	69%	88%	132%	79%	78%	144%
	Essential expenses % of net income	44%	59%	123%	69%	68%	126%
	Debt % of net income	16%	24%	0%	0%	0%	0%
	Year end Checking & savings accounts	$ 65,927	$ 30,175	$ 16,819	$ 32,499	$ 49,392	$ 29,377
	Checking & Saving months of expense coverage	14.8	5.1	3.7	6.5	9.7	5.4

Was this the only option they had? No. As I said we ran multiple scenarios which gave them greater confidence in the viability of their plan and strategies. We found more than one approach that would work.

Just because we had a set of strategies and initiatives does not ensure plan execution. Many things can change within a year, let alone five years. When the children would be born was a major assumption in the cash flow model. Every time a family grows, uncertainty increases with future expense planning.

Is it a perfect plan? There is no such thing when you are looking out five years. Is the plan sensible?

We believe so, but do not lose sleep worrying about it. John and Mary will focus on plan execution for the next year, and we will refine it again the following year—sooner if a major unplanned event surfaces.

Tim

Tim was fifty-four, single, never married, had no children, and had paid off his home mortgage. He lived well within his means. He participated in his employer's pretax investment 401(k) plan. He took two modest vacations each year to the beach just hours from his home. His hobbies and interests were attending music, art, and other social events. He paid cash for his vehicles and had no debt. His home was twenty-two years old but maintained in good condition. He intended to live in his home throughout his retirement years. His vehicle was eight years old, and he wanted to replace it in the next two years. He also wanted to do some modest property improvements in the next eight years before he retired.

Postretirement, he wanted to make sure that financial stress would be minimized. He wanted to take four vacations each year and do some bigger upgrades to his home and furniture over time. He wanted to increase his entertainment expenses and replace his vehicle every ten years.

He wanted me to help him understand if retiring at age sixty-three would be sensible. Below is the quality-of-life plan he created.

Tim Quality of Life Plan

Quality of Life Plan	Strategies	Initiatives
Single & Employed		
Enjoy time with family and friends	Validate retirement at age 63 is rational.	Rationalize investment contributions for future years until retirement, plan future expenses for home, cars, and other, Buil cash flow forecast and contingency funds availability.
Pursue hobbies / interest.		
Take two vacations each year.		
Retired		
Retire at age 63.	Minimize financial stress.	Build cash flow analysis post retirement until age 95, plan future post retirement expenses for home, cars, and other, forecast expenses coverage funds availability.
Take 4 vacations each year		
Enjoy time with family and friends.		
Upgrade home - kitchen & furniture		

We began where every client starts. He organized his income, investment balances, and checking and savings balances for January 1 of the current year. Next, we forecasted his annual expenses for the current year. Below is a summary of his current-year financial snapshot.

Tim Financial Example

		Current Year Begin
	Year begin combined checking & savings	**$ 48,000**
	Year Begin Pre-Tax Investment Plan balance	**$ 513,000**
	Gross Income	$ 85,000
	Average Bonus Income	$ 6,375
	Total Gross Income	$ 91,375
	Contribution to Pre-tax Investment Plan	$ 13,706
	Net income after all withholdings	$ 58,461
Expense Type	**Annual Expenses**	
Essential	Housing expenses - taxes, utilities, upkeep, insurance, other	$ 7,706
Essential	Transportation - fuel, repairs, insurance	$ 4,500
Essential	Other Insurance & Health Care	$ 1,925
Essential	Groceries	$ 10,400
Discretionary	Clothes	$ 1,000
Discretionary	Entertainment - vacations, spending money, holidays	$ 5,400
Discretionary	All other	$ 1,150
	Total	**$ 32,081**
	Net Income minus expenses (cash flow)	**$ 26,380**
	Expenses % of net income	55%
	Essential expenses % of net income	42%
	Year end Checking & savings accounts	$ 74,380
	Checking & Saving months of expenses coverage - year end	27.8

Tim's financial ratios were excellent. His expenses were a modest percentage of his net income. His contingency funds were adequate. His investment plan balance was over a half million dollars. We would pursue the following game plan to gain insight into his key question: "Can, or should, I retire at age sixty-three?"

The following steps are to be taken to manage today forward until ten years postretirement:

1. We would build a cash flow outlook ten years postretirement using expenses with inflation factors we believed to be reasonable for the next eighteen years (ten years postretirement). Next, we would run inflation sensitivity analysis.
2. We would rationalize and include future one-off expenses for car replacements, home projects, and other needs.
3. We would test multiple future years' contribution scenarios to his pretax investment account and average rate of return.
4. We would estimate his Social Security annual amount using his latest Social Security statement, assuming an average 2.5 percent future years COLA adjustment (the past thirty-year COLA increase average).
5. Tim would then pick the inflation rate (2.8 percent), average annual wage increase (3 percent), and average annual rate of return on his investment plan (7.5 percent) he wanted to use in the refined cash flow outlook. We did not use a linear inflation factor (2.8 percent) for each expense. Some costs such as insurance, health care, groceries, and entertainment used higher values, while other expenses such as cell phones,

cable television, and home taxes used lower values.

6. We calculated taxes for each year during his retirement using current-year tax tables and will refine these values in the future as tax regulations change.

Below is a summary of the outlook created for Tim:

1. Tim's current contribution percentage to his pretax 401(k) investment plan was not going to comfortably enable his quality-of-life plan during retirement. He would need to increase his contributions to his pretax investment plan or delay retirement by two to three years to reduce risks.
2. After increasing his future years' contributions to his employer pretax investment account to take advantage of the catch-up contribution for people age fifty and up, Tim would have $1,270,000 at age sixty-three, his first year of retirement. His checking and savings balance would be $132,000 after accounting for the one-off future expenses for cars and home upgrades preretirement.
3. We further increased certain expenses (e.g., vacations, entertainment, and furniture upgrades) because his cash flows were sufficient.

4. His investment account would be just shy of $2,000,000 in year ten postretirement. His checking and savings account balance ten years postretirement would be $67,000, providing more than a year of contingency expenses coverage. We did not allow contingency funds to drop below six months of annual expenses for any given year.

The following steps are to be taken to manage postretirement until age ninety-five:

1. We wanted to build the cash flow model out to age ninety-five to have a conservative life expectancy assumption.
2. We wanted to refine one-off expenses for vehicles, home upgrades, and home repairs until age ninety-five. Then we would evaluate his discretionary expenses to explore opportunities to enrich his quality-of-life plan (e.g., vacations, spending money, hobbies and interests) without adding significant risk to his plan.
3. We wanted to run sensitivity analyses on both the inflation factors and annual rate of return in the cash flow model.

    a. What does the cash flow model outlook say through age ninety-five with future one-off expenses added?

b. If we had a major marketplace correction (35 percent drop in his pretax investment plan the first year Tim retired and no recovery for four years), how would that affect his cash flow outlook?
c. If inflation doubled versus the assumed rate we used in the original assumptions, what would be the cash flow impact?

Below is a summary of the outlook until age ninety-five:

1. We rationalized home maintenance and upgrade expenses for the thirty-two years postretirement (e.g., kitchen remodel, roofs, driveways, windows, heating and air conditioning, appliances, paint, landscaping, and furniture, among others). Adjusted for inflation, this added just over $250,000 to his postretirement expenses. We laid out expenses to replace his vehicles every ten years, which added another $225,000 of expenses. We juggled these expenses in future years to optimize his cash flows. After adding just shy of a half million dollars of future expenses, Tim still had a cash flow strategy that would support him living to age ninety-five. At age ninety-five, he still had over a million dollars in his investment account.

2. With a 35 percent drop in Tim's pretax investment plan the first year of retirement and no marketplace recovery for four years, we still had a cash flow model that would support him until ninety-five.
3. We ran sensitivity analysis on our inflation assumptions to test the impact on our cash flow model. If inflation doubled over our model assumption, Tim would run out of money at age ninety-one. We were somewhat dismissive of this impact because we could always pull back on discretionary expenses if necessary in the future (e.g., home upgrades, vehicles, entertainment, and vacations, among others)) without a significant impact on his quality-of-life plan. In addition, we did not increase the plan COLA adjustment average of 2.5 percent annually during his retirement. If, in fact, inflation did double, those COLA adjustments should be higher than our plan assumptions, improving our cash flow outlook.

Tim now had a financial outlook that supported is quality-of-life plan. His strategies were tested and refined.

His focus would now change to managing his expenses and investment contributions each year until retirement. We would update the model every year or two unless major unknowns surfaced that required updates that are more frequent.

A year later (year two of his plan), Tim was right on pace with the cash flow model we built, same with his pretax investment plan. In year three, he was modestly behind on his pretax investment rate of return plan but on pace with his cash flow plans. In year four, his pretax investment average annual rate of return had slightly exceeded our plan values; and his cash flow plan was better than our initial plan, as he did not spend as much money for home upgrades as we forecast.

Ongoing coaching discussions encouraged Tim to get his living will complete and think about wealth pass-on strategies, the benefits of forming a trust, and future investment strategies once he retired and his 401(k) transitioned to an IRA. We discussed how and when to build his advisor team. We are now starting to refine our tax strategies to support those years when we need higher cash from his investment portfolio to cover those one-off future expenses and minimize the taxes related to required minimum distributions.

Case Studies Summary

The above case studies are examples that I often encounter when new clients engage me. They have done a good job of managing their debt and spending but lack alignment of strategies and initiatives to enable their quality-of-life plan longer term. Unintentionally, they risk creating conflicts that will derail their plans.

Closing Summary

You can make a lot of money and not have a high quality of life.

You can have a high quality of life and make a modest amount of money.

Do not chase financial targets unless you align them to enable your quality-of-life plan.

If you have a plan, it must be dynamic so you can adjust for change and the unexpected.

If you have a plan without clearly defined strategies to accomplish it, you are depending on good luck to achieve it.

If you have strategies defined, you need key initiatives to support them.

If you have a quality-of-life plan, meaningful strategies and initiatives, and a dynamic or renewable mindset, you must be the champion of the plan execution.

A champion of their quality-of-life plan will be committed to continuing education and a continuous improvement planning process. They never allow others to control their strategies.

To be a successful champion of your quality-of-life plan, you must let go of the idea that you are in control of all outcomes in your life's journey.

The unexpected is coming; when it does, your job is to adjust. I have rebuilt businesses that have burned down or suffered major damage by earthquakes, tornadoes, and hurricanes. Dreadful things happen to good businesses and to good people.

Having a team of advisors (financial coach, financial advisor, tax professional, insurance professionals, and legal team) to assist and educate yourself will be valuable in your journey.

What do you want to look back and say about your life's journey on your last day on earth? That is the culmination of your quality-of-life plan.

Testimonial

Working with Quality-of-life Financial Planning has been a transformative experience for my retirement planning. They did not just focus on the numbers—they took the time to understand my lifestyle, goals, and dreams for the future.

They crafted a personalized plan that not only secures my financial future but also enhances my quality of life. Thanks to their expertise and thoughtful approach, I am now more confident than ever about the years ahead. I could not recommend them more highly!

Mike G, age 44, TN

With retirement fast approaching and having worked with a trusted financial advisor for many years, my comfort level with my planning was short of complete confidence. Engaging with Quality-of-life Financial Planning turned out to be just what I was looking for, (i.e., setting a retirement date with renewed confidence that my plan will indeed fulfill all my quality-of-life objectives). The process was quick and simple. The coaching feedback was compelling and encouraged constructive fine-tuning of my financial strategies. They provided valuable feedback on my Family Trust, tax strategies, retirement expenses and other planning considerations. I would highly recommend the Quality-of-Life Financial Planning process.

Bob L, age 68, OH

Quality-of-Life Financial Planning renewed my confidence that I can achieve my goals. I have been tracking my expenses for many years on an app. After my initial plan review and follow up coaching calls, I refined my strategies moving forward. I was amazed with the personalized coaching feedback I received. The value exceeded my expectations. I would and have recommended them to others.

Jane S, age 37, SC

I was nearing retirement and uncertain if I had enough money to reach my goals. Quality-of-Life Financial Planning guided me through an initial outlook of reaching my age 62, retirement goal. I was surprised how simple the process was and amazed how informative the output reports were. After the coaching and refinements to my financial plans, I had a renewed confidence that I could retire when I wanted and reach my quality-of-life goals, Dan guided me on important other financial consideration that were not on my radar screen. I would highly recommend Quality-of-Life Financial Planning. I will be using them every year moving forward to refine and adjust my plans as necessary.

Mitch F. age 54, MS.

I have used Quality-of-Life Financial Planning for 10-plus years. They assisted me with financial strategies to evaluate and reach my quality-of-life goals. This includes IRAs, Pensions, Annuities, CDs, 401K, and Roth IRAs. They refined my cash flow strategies and saved me thousands of dollars a year in taxes. I retired at age 63 and live a better lifestyle than when I was employed. I will continue to use them to refine my quality-of-life goals throughout retirement. I would highly recommend them to anyone who is serious about creating a longer-term financial vison that aligns to your unique quality-of-life goals.

Don H, age 66, OH

I am in my early twenties, employed, and started investing money for the future through my employer plan. I engaged Quality-of-Life Financial Planning to help me build a long-term financial outlook and understand financial strategies.

The process was simple, and the coaching feedback I received gave me valuable direction and confidence. I will be renewing my plans every year to make sure I stay on track. I would recommend them to anyone who wants a plan that enable their quality-of-life goals.

Alexis B, age 23, TN

Financial security is a priority for anyone approaching retirement, or, in my case, someone who's already there. "Quality of Life" provided a broad look at planning for what the future holds for me, and my family. Mapping out future expenses, such as house upgrades, vehicle purchases, travel, inflation adjustments, and insurance costs, gives me a true sense of just how far my money will go for decades to come.

I would urge anyone who is feeling unsure about their financial future both before, and in preparing for retirement, to participate in a "Quality of Life" analysis.

Bill L, age 64, Ohio

About the Author

Dan Corbin is the owner and president of DRC Consulting LLC, a firm whose Quality-of-Life Financial Planning division helps individuals align their finances with their life goals. A retired executive vice president of a Fortune 1000 company, Corbin brings over forty-six years of operations management experience to his consulting practice, including extensive work in business plan development and continuous improvement initiatives as a member of executive leadership teams.

For decades, Corbin has applied the same strategic discipline he used to drive results in the corporate world to help clients build and execute their personal quality-of-life plans. His approach centers on aligning strategies and initiatives to a clear plan, then tracking performance to stay proactive through every stage of life. This book distills that decades-long process into a practical, life-cycle framework for readers.

www.ingramcontent.com/pod-product-compliance
Lightning Source LLC
LaVergne TN
LVHW090431210926
848480LV00002B/775
9798898881177